The WELSH 3000ft P

Photographs by
Bruce Herrod

Text and captions by
Sue Thompson

DIAL
PRESS

First published 1994

ISBN 0 7110 2291 7

© Bruce Herrod 1994

Designed by Geoffrey Wadsley

Published by Dial Press

an imprint of Ian Allan Ltd, Terminal House, Station Approach, Shepperton, Surrey TW17 8AS; and printed by Ian Allan Printing Ltd, Coombelands House, Coombelands Lane, Addlestone, Weybridge, Surrey KT15 1HY.

Front cover:
Walkers scrambling up the east ridge to the summit of Crib Goch (3,028ft/923m).

Title Page:
Llyn Ogwen frozen in late winter from the north ridge of Tryfan (3,002ft/915m). Elidir Fawr (3,031ft/924m) lies in the far distance and Y Garn (3,106ft/947m) on the left.

Opposite:
The Snowdon massif viewed across the still waters of Llynau Mymbyr. This is the heart of Snowdonia (Eryri in Welsh), encompassing three of the 3,000ft peaks (Snowdon, left; Crib Goch, centre and Carnedd Ugain, right).

Introduction

The Welsh 3,000ft peaks of the Snowdon massif, the Glyderau and Carneddau ranges constitute the heart of Snowdonia, a unique blend of geology, legend and natural beauty. To grasp the mystery of these mountains, look no further than their names: Yr Wyddfa (*The Tomb*), the summit of Snowdon where, local legend has it, King Arthur slew the giant, Rita Gawr; Yr Elen (*Hill of the Fawn*), which harks back centuries to when hillsides were thickly wooded hunting grounds, and Castell y Gwynt (*Castle of the Winds*) whose spiked stone formations between Glyder Fawr and Glyder Fach, speak of geological aeons.

The history of man's presence in the mountains of Snowdonia pales into insignificance compared to the age of the land itself. In Cambrian times (600 million years ago) Snowdonia was on the floor of a great ocean. Sedimentary rocks were laid down over the next 200 million years, while volcanoes erupted producing lava and ash. Then, the rock strata were uplifted and, after a period of erosion, folded and tilted into the sort of configuration seen today. Extensive glaciation during the last Ice Age, 10,000 years ago, defined many of the cwms and valleys, such as Cwm Idwal and the Llanberis Pass.

Walkers today witness the forces of geology first hand each time they scramble up the great pyramid of Tryfan, or see the rock strata of Yr Wyddfa etched in a light dusting of snow. The Romans, not content with mere observation, mined the region for its copper, a tradition revived by local inhabitants in the 18th century. Meanwhile slate, long used as an essential roofing material in Wales, continues to be quarried near Llanberis and Bethesda.

In Welsh legend, King Arthur is closely associated with these parts, having fought his last battle on the Bwlch-y-Saethau (*Pass of Arrows*) between Yr Wyddfa and Lliwedd. Afterwards, so the story goes, the Knights of the Round Table retreated to a cave below Lliwedd to wait in slumber for their king to rise again. In the realm of history, however, medieval Welsh princes like Llewelyn the Great almost certainly took refuge with their flocks in the mountains during times of war, which continued long after the death of Llewelyn the Last in 1282, and the conquest of Gwynedd by Edward I.

The Ogwen Valley, the main thoroughfare of the A5 today, was a forbidding and extremely isolated region for much of its history. Permanent farm settlements were established only in the 15-16th centuries, when traffic was mostly four-legged. The first real outsiders to disturb the peace of the locals arrived in the 17th century: botanists and geologists drawn to the mountains out of scientific curiosity, not an intrinsic love of wild places.

Indeed, not all famous visitors of the past took kindly to the sort of broody skies and inhospitable winds that can still send walkers scurrying for cover today: 'This horrid spot of hills,' was how Edmond Halley, of comet fame, described these parts when he climbed Snowdon in 1697 in the name of scientific experimentation.

After Thomas Pennant published *Journey to Snowdon* in 1781, those drawn to the mountains for their own sake began to arrive in greater numbers. Tourism, which began with a period of road building under the direction of Thomas Telford between 1800 and 1830, grew significantly with the railways. In 1896 a railway line up Snowdon itself

was finally opened. The Pen-y-Gwyrd Hotel below Pen-y-Pass has now been home to walkers and climbers for nearly two centuries. And more recent institutions too, such as the Idwal Youth Hostel and Plas-y-Brenin National Mountaineering Centre at Capel Curig, have become just as much part of the landscape as the hills themselves.

The idea of traversing the Welsh 3,000ft peaks in one go was probably first conceived in Victorian days. Early this century, walkers in full tweeds and heavy boots could take as long as 24 hours to cover the distance from the summit of Snowdon in the south to Foel Fras in the north. These days, however, a good fell runner can complete the traverse in well under 5 hours. But take your time to admire the mountains and lakes cradled in glaciated cwms. Why rush? From the dragon-scales of Tryfan and the knife edge of Crib Goch to the grassy expanses of the Carneddau – where you can wander in virtual solitude with only the sheep for company – there are 3,000ft peaks to suit everyone.

Although man scarcely registers on Snowdonia's geological timescale, his short presence has left disproportionately large scars on parts of the landscape. Given time these can heal, as testified by the now barely discernible vestiges of the copper mines in the shadow of Snowdon that flourished until 1913. But the new steps of the Upper Pyg Track above Glaslyn show only too clearly the pressures of modern tourism: footpath-rebuilding is now a high priority in key areas of the Snowdonia National Park. Indeed, The National Trust, which owns Cwm Idwal, Tryfan and much of the Glyderau range – where many of the most seriously eroded footpaths are to be found – launched a Snowdonia appeal in 1990 under the chairmanship of Sir Anthony Hopkins. Funds raised are aiding a comprehensive range of conservation work.

Down in the valleys, traffic too is considerably heavier than early last century when Thomas Telford was commissioned to build what is now the A5. Whether this key road should be widened to improve safety and access remains an issue of dogged debate between locals, representatives of the tourist industry and the Welsh authorities. After all, the trend in numbers continues ever upwards: an estimated 12 million people now visit the Snowdonia National Park annually, of which about 500,000 climb Snowdon. How many is too many?

'North Wales is thronged this summer by tourists. Snowdon is ascended by everyone because it is the highest top,' comments one visitor. The irony is that his words were uttered not recently, but back in the mid-19th century – proof, perhaps, that all perceptions are relative. The reality, fortunately, is that the Welsh 3,000ft peaks continue to embody some of Britain's finest and wildest scenery. Savour their age-old grandeur, but tread gently.

Opposite:
Study of Elidir Fawr (3,031ft/924m): The Bwlch y Brechan, seen along the bottom of the picture here, is the point where Llwybr yr Offeiriad (*The Priest's Path*) ran over the flanks of Elidir Fawr from the church in the village of Nant Peris. Clergymen, it is believed, walked this path in summer as early as the 15th century in order to hold church services for the locals *en route*. From this high point it descended to Tŷ Gwyn and crossed the Ogwen River before turning north to Moel Faban near Bethesda and Aber on the coast.

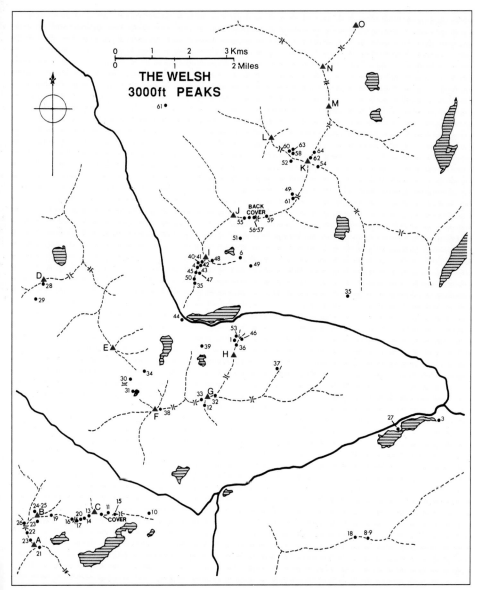

THE WELSH 3000ft PEAKS

The Welsh 3,000ft Peaks

Snowdon massif:

A.	Snowdon	3,560ft	1,085m
B.	Carnedd Ugain	3,494ft	1,065m
C.	Crib Goch	3,028ft	923m

The Glyderau range:

D.	Elidir Fawr	3,031ft	924m
E.	Y Garn	3,106ft	947m
F.	Glyder Fawr	3,278ft	999m
G.	Glyder Fach	3,261ft	994m
H.	Tryfan	3,002ft	915m

The Carneddau range:

I.	Pen yr Ole Wen	3,209ft	978m
J.	Carnedd Dafydd	3,425ft	1,044m
K.	Carnedd Llewelyn	3,491ft	1,064m
L.	Yr Elen	3,156ft	962m
M.	Foel Grach	3,202ft	976m
N.	Garnedd Uchaf	3,038ft	926m
O.	Foel Fras	3,091ft	942m

Metric heights taken from O.S. Outdoor Leisure Map no. 17 (Snowdonia – Snowdon & Conwy Valley areas, 1:25,000). Imperial equivalents given in feet.

Opposite:
Rocks at the outflow of Ffynnon Lloer (*Lake of the Moon*) beneath Pen yr Ole Wen (*Hill of the White Light*, left) and Carnedd Dafydd rising behind. Since World War 2, a number of pilots flying down the Ogwen Valley have crashed in bad visibility on these innocent-looking scree slopes. Pieces of metal can still be found on the hillside and are also visible beneath the waters of the lake.

Left:
A panorama of the Snowdon massif viewed from Moel Siabod (2,860ft/872m) near Capel Curig: 'Perhaps in the whole world there is no more picturesquely beautiful region than Snowdon, a region of mountains, lakes, cataracts and groves, in which Nature shows herself in her most grand and beautiful forms,' wrote George Borrow in *Wild Wales*, published in 1862. The hotel at Pen-y-Gwyrd (bottom right) was a small inn in Borrow's day, and has been home to generations of walkers and mountaineers. Members of Sir John Hunt's successful 1953 Everest team based themselves here during training. The ceiling of the bar is still adorned with their signatures.

Right:
Stormy weather brewing over the Llanberis Pass, which leads to the twin lakes of Llyn Peris and Llyn Padarn, both named after saints. Nature in this primeval tract of giant boulders and inhospitable crags was not tamed easily. It is possible that the Romans, who conquered North Wales in AD 78, may have used a route through the pass, but it was more or less inaccessible until around 1830 when a proper road was finally built. The end of the valley shows the U-shape typical of glacial action during the last Ice Age.

Opposite:
Reward for a demanding scramble up the east ridge of Crib Goch (*Red Ridge*): view back towards Llyn Cwmffynon (ffynnon means spring or well). The A4086 from Caernarfon to Capel Curig snakes up the Llanberis Pass and over Pen-y-Pass, its highest point, site of one of the busiest car parks in Snowdonia. At weekends, hundreds of walkers set out from here for a day in the Snowdon massif.

Right:
Floating in the clouds: Crib Goch (left) with Snowdon behind viewed from Castell y Gwynt (*Castle of the Winds*) situated on the Bwlch y Ddwy Glyder (*Pass of the two Glyders*). On a majestic winter's day like this, negotiating Crib Goch can become a full scale mountaineering expedition and should only be attempted with proper equipment and experience.

Above left:
Walking the knife-edge of Crib Goch (3,028ft/923m) with Carnedd Ugain (*Cairn of Twenty*, 3,494ft/1,065m), as the summit of Crib-y-Ddysgl is correctly known, behind. Yr Wyddfa (summit of Snowdon, 3,560ft/1,085m) is on the left. This route poses a real challenge for those of a nervous disposition, but those with a head for heights find it highly satisfying.

Below left:
Striding out on Crib Goch requires careful concentration, even in perfect weather. In the background, separated from the Snowdon massif by the Llanberis Pass, lie the Glyderau: on the left, in shadow, is Glyder Fawr (3,278ft/999m), while the peak in the centre is Glyder Fach (3,261ft/994m).

Left:
View from half way up the east ridge of Crib Goch looking over the north ridge towards Elidir Fawr (3,031ft/924m, left), Y Garn (3,106ft/947m, in shadow on the right) and Carnedd y Filiast (*Cairn of the Female Greyhound*) in the centre background, so called after the greyhound, symbol of Ceridwen, the Welsh goddess of nature. The mass of rock below Y Garn is known as Esgair Felen.

Opposite:
Landscape of eternal shadows: view towards the twin lakes of Llyn Peris and Llyn Padarn from the pinnacles of Crib Goch, with Llyn Glas in the foreground. Down in the valley, the small village of Nant Peris nestles amongst green fields. Rising up the shoulder of Elidir Fawr are the slate quarries of Llanberis. Slate, which has been used in Snowdonia since Roman times, was first quarried commercially in the second half of the 18th century.

Right:
Safely over the pinnacles of Crib Goch: walkers arrive at the reassuringly broad Bwlch Coch, (*Red Col*) after a fine autumn scramble over the most exposed ridge of all the Welsh 3,000ft peaks.

Opposite:
Setting out from Bwlch Coch up the ridge of Crib-y-Ddysgl to the summit of Carnedd Ugain (3,494ft/1,065m). To the left the Pyg Track, which is joined by the Miners' Track above Glaslyn (*Blue Lake*), wends its way up to Bwlch Glas (*Blue Pass*), where the path which comes up the other side from Llanberis also converges. Yr Wyddfa, Snowdon's rocky summit (3,560ft/1,085m) is on the left.

Left:
The meaning of Crib-y-Ddysgl, *Edge of the Dish,* is beautifully portrayed here, as walkers survey the massive sweep of rock before them *en route* to Crib Goch. What constitutes a magnificent scramble along here in summer can become a major expedition in icy or wintry conditions. Not many walkers tackle the Snowdon Horseshoe clockwise like this so as to avoid the steep descent of Crib Goch's east ridge.

Opposite:
View from Moel Siabod (2,860ft/872m) of the Snowdon massif. The bulky summit of Snowdon (3,560ft/1,085m, centre) is flanked on the left by Y Lliwedd (2,947ft/898m) and on the right by Carnedd Ugain (3,494ft/1,065m) and Crib Goch (3,028ft/923m). The traverse of all these peaks, including Y Lliwedd, is known as the Snowdon Horseshoe, often described as one of the finest ridge walks in the British Isles. Walkers normally start from Pen Y Pass, completing the round in an anticlockwise direction. Also clearly visible is the pipeline which runs from the reservoir of Llyn Llydaw to the Cwm Dyli hydro-electric generating station in the Upper Gwynant Valley.

Right:
Glaslyn and the Clogwyn y Garnedd face of Snowdon viewed from the col of Bwlch Coch between Crib Goch and Carnedd Ugain. The vibrant green-blue hue of Glaslyn is caused by the copper content of the rocks beneath. Although the Romans (and probably local tribes before them) were the first to mine copper here, the heyday of commercial mining was the 19th century. According to local folklore, Glaslyn is both bottomless and haunted.

Opposite:
View from Yr Wyddfa (summit of Snowdon) of Llyn Llydaw, with Moel Siabod in the distance. Originally boats were used to transport men and mining equipment across the lake to and from the copper works higher up at Glaslyn. A causeway was first built in 1853, but flooded frequently. Now Llyn Llydaw is a reservoir with a pipeline that runs to a small power station in the Upper Gwynant Valley.

Opposite:
View from near Bwlch Glas looking back over Glaslyn towards the reservoir of Llyn Llydaw. The Pyg Track is three miles long and starts from Pen-y-Pass. As the newly restored upper trail here shows, keeping the most heavily used footpaths in good repair is a high priority within the Snowdonia National Park.

Above left:
Yr Wyddfa, the summit of England and Wales: a light dusting of snow highlights rock strata laid down during the Ordovician Period (500 million years ago) which were uplifted in the late Silurian Period (395 million years ago). Indeed, fossils of crustacea found in these rocks confirm that Snowdon once lay on the sea

Above right:
Walkers approach the summit of Snowdon along the railway tracks. The route over Crib Goch, the Pyg and Miners' Tracks, and the route from Llanberis Pass all converge here. The railway was officially opened on 6 April 1896 after a total investment of £76,000. Nowadays, of the half a million annual visitors to the summit of Snowdon, approximately three-quarters walk up and one-quarter arrive by train.

Left:
Early winter snow dusts the top slopes of Parsley Fern Gully, viewed from Carnedd Ugain. The railway to the summit of Snowdon from the village of Llanberis follows the Llechog ridge (centre right). In the near distance is Llyn Padarn, the village of Llanberis itself and the Menai Strait with Anglesey beyond. The Llanberis slate quarries are visible on the right, a grey scar across the landscape. On closer inspection, however, Llanberis slate is far from dull in appearance, ranging in colour from distinctive blues to reds.

Left:
Sunset over the Snowdon massif (from left to right: Snowdon, Crib Goch, Carnedd Ugain) across the Mymbyr Lakes evokes all the romance of Arthurian legend: the col to the left of Snowdon is the Bwlch-y-Saethau (*Pass of Arrows*) where King Arthur is said to have fought his last battle.

Opposite:
Study in green: Clogwyn Llechwedd Llo leads to the angular ridge in the foreground of Moel y Cynghorion (*Hill of Councillors*, 2,211ft/674m). The ridge then continues across two further grassy tops to Moel Eilio (2,382ft/726m), thought to be named after some ancient chieftain, in the background. Behind lies the end of the Menai Strait and Anglesey.

Right:
The heavens close in on the summit of Elidir Fawr (3,031ft/924m) at the northern end of the Glyderau. Elidir, the English son-in-law of Maelgwm, Prince of Gwynedd, attempted to claim the right of succession to his father-in-law, but died in battle. Thus Elidir Fawr was known originally as Carnedd Elidir, after a memorial cairn built by his followers. Deep in the recesses of the mountain these days is the pumping station of a hydro-electric power scheme that uses the waters of Marchlyn Mawr reservoir.

Opposite:
Sunlight strikes the hillside above the village of Nant Peris at the foot of the Llanberis Pass, viewed from the slopes of Elidir Fawr. The normally distinctive silhouette of Crib Goch (left) and Carnedd Ugain (head in the clouds) in the distance is less familiar from this angle. It was from the village of Nant Peris, where the church dates from the 14th or early 15th century, that Llwybr yr Offeiriad (*The Priest's Path*) ran over the flanks of Elidir Fawr *en route* to Tŷ Gwyn and the Ogwen River.

Left:
Evening sun on Llyn y Cŵn (*Lake of Dogs*) which nestles between Glyder Fawr and Y Garn. The name of the lake probably derives from hounds that were once used in deer hunting on the hills here. There is a direct path this way from the head of Llyn Ogwen to Nant Peris in the Llanberis Valley.

Opposite:
The easiest route to the summit of Y Garn (*The Rock,* centre) lies straight across this stream that flows from Llyn y Cŵn down through the cliffs of Devil's Kitchen beneath. From this flattened angle, Y Garn (3,106ft/947m) gives little hint of its shapely silhouette often described as an armchair when viewed from the other side of the Ogwen valley.

Right:
The Cantilever Rock on the summit plateau of Glyder Fach (3,261ft/994m) has been a favourite with walkers throughout the ages. The tradition is to balance one's way along this massive slab of granite weighing many tons to check how solid it is. One of the earliest illustrations of the Cantilever is found in Thomas Pennant's late 18th century book, *Tours in Wales.*

Opposite:
Winter paradise: view over the rock formations of Castell y Gwynt (*Castle of the Winds*) towards the Snowdon massif engulfed in banks of cloud. Castell y Gwynt, which dominates Bwlch y Ddwy Glyder (*Pass of the two Glyders*), is one of Snowdonia's most distinctive features, comprising frost-shattered boulders that lean like neglected gravestones.

Right:
View from Twll Du (*Black Hole*), more popularly known as Devil's Kitchen, towards Llyn Idwal (*Idwal's Lake*) and Pen yr Ole Wen (3,209ft/978m). In the 12th century, legend has it, Idwal, son of Owain, a Prince of Gwynedd, was drowned in the lake by a jealous relative. Much later, in 1831, Charles Darwin and Professor Adam Sedgwick searched its shores for fossils. So absorbing was their hunt that only years later did Darwin write about Cwm Idwal's glaciated features, noting its moraines and shattered boulders, remnants of the last Ice Age 10,000 years ago. Cwm Idwal is now a nature reserve and a Site of Special Scientific Interest (SSSI).

Above left:
Silhouette of Tryfan (3,002ft/915m) enhanced by moon rise: no Welsh 3,000ft peak is quite as immediately recognisable as Tryfan's dragon-back, which rises from the floor of the Ogwen Valley. The two summit pinnacles of Adam & Eve are just visible (top centre).

Below left:
This view of Y Garn (3,106ft/947m) and Cwm Idwal from Pen yr Ole Wen (3,209ft/ 978m) shows perfectly the two ridges framing Cwm Clyd (*Sheltered Hollow*), which give the mountain its appearance of an armchair. Both ridges provide shorter but steeper ascents than the route directly behind Llyn Idwal underneath Devil's Kitchen. A light dusting of snow covers the slopes that rise from Llyn y Cŵn to Glyder Fawr.

Right:
A great day out scrambling up the north ridge of Tryfan across layers of lava and marine shale. This is one of the more difficult routes that crisscross this most satisfying of Welsh 3,000ft peaks. In the valley far below is the farm of Gwern Gof Uchaf (*The Smith by the Alders*) and Little Tryfan, a good rock face for climbing practice.

Opposite:
Viewed from Braich y Ddeugwm, the north ridge (right skyline) of Tryfan (3,002ft/915m) thrusts upwards from the Ogwen Valley. It looks more formidable from afar than close to (see left) but offers an exhilarating scramble nonetheless. There are several rock-climbing routes up the east face to the South Peak, Main Peak (with Adam & Eve pinnacles) and North Peak. The col on the left is the Bwlch-y-Tryfan, over which the old Miners' Track passed from Llyn Ogwen via Pen-y-Gwyrd to Glaslyn beneath Snowdon.

Left:
In the depths of winter, just near the footpath as it descends from Bwlch-y-Tryfan, route of the Miners' Track, a semi-frozen mountain stream struggles to bubble on its way from Llyn Bochlwyd to Llyn Ogwen.

Opposite:
Flowers of ice adorn frost-shattered rocks on Glyder Fawr (3,278ft/999m). Although Glyder Fawr is 5 metres higher than Glyder Fach, its sister summit, it tends to be less popular with visitors. In the distance, the Snowdon massif sits under skies that threaten more snow.

Right:
The first road to open up Nant Ffrancon, gateway to Snowdonia from Bethesda, was built on the west side of the valley in 1792 by Richard Pennant, the great industrialist. The A5 today (right) runs on the east side, following Thomas Telford's original 19th century route. Above the Penrhyn slate quarries (right, background), rises the Atlantic Slab on the flanks of Carnedd y Filiast (left, background) distinctive for its great ripples of Cambrian rock over 500 million years old.

Opposite:
According to a map dating from 1768, Pentre, (bottom centre, viewed here from Pen yr Ole Wen) once owned the whole of Cwm Idwal. Although Pentre is a working farm today, its name means 'village', suggesting that it constituted a collection of buildings at one time. However, landslides caused by mining in the late 18th century resulted in devastation on at least one occasion. The building today dates from the 19th century.

Right:
Rhaeadr Ogwen (Ogwen Falls)
is situated next to the A5 at the
western end of Llyn Ogwen.
Nearby is Ogwen Cottage (first
used by holiday-makers and
climbers over a century ago
and now a training centre for
the Birmingham Local
Education Authority) and
Idwal Youth Hostel. Above the
falls was a mill for shaping
hone, or oil, stones (used to
sharpen tools) which were
much in demand during the
period of road building in the
early 19th century. There was
also a forge here.

Left:
Natural rock sculpture on the shoulder of Pen yr Ole Wen (3,209ft/978m), looking towards Foel Goch with Elidir Fawr (3,031ft/924m) behind. This route, a straight ascent of Pen yr Ole Wen starting from the Ogwen Falls, is one of the hardest ways to reach the Carneddau but offers a magnificent panorama along the entire Ogwen Valley. Foel Goch is one of the commonest mountain names in Wales, simply meaning *Red Hill*.

Left:
Ascending the south ridge of
Pen yr Ole Wen with Llyn
Ogwen behind: from the A5
this route offers direct, but
steep access over rocky ground
to the Carneddau range, as well
as tremendous views back
towards Tryfan and the
Glyderau on the other side of
the valley.

Opposite:
Winter loosens its grip on the
Ogwen Valley and the farm of
Gwern Gof Uchaf. The slabby
rock outcrop of Little Tryfan
(foreground) has been used by
generations of climbing begin-
ners. To the left of the A5 is
Pen yr Helgi Du (*Hill of the
Black Hound*) with Pen Llithrig
y Wrach (*Slippery Hill of the
Witch*) behind.

48

Right:
Early morning frost clings to the shadows beside Ffynnon Lloer (*Lake of the Moon*) in Cwm Lloer beneath Pen yr Ole Wen (3,209ft/978m). This picturesque name is said to hark back to an old superstition that it was lucky to obtain the first view of the new moon from a high vantage point. Pieces of metal wreckage are sometimes visible in the water from old planes whose pilots were unlucky enough to crash on the surrounding slopes.

Above left:
The Carneddau range running along the skyline (summit of Carnedd Dafydd, 3,425ft/1,044m, centre) is most easily reached via the path from the A5 at the eastern end of Llyn Ogwen. There are no fantastic rock formations here, only sheep and walkers, but the wild, grassy expanses have their own charm. Carnedd Dafydd is believed to be named after Dafydd, younger son of Llewelyn the Great (1194-1240).

Below left:
The ascent to the summit of Carnedd Llewelyn (3,491ft/1,064m) from Bwlch Cyfryw-drum (*Pass of the Saddle Ridge*). Llewelyn the Great himself, after whom the mountain is probably named, is said to have used the summit as an observation post. Old cairns also hark back to medieval days when cattle and sheep were driven up here for protection in times of war.

Left:
Moss-covered rocks by
Ffynnon Lloer nestling beneath
Pen yr Ole Wen. The dampness
of Snowdonia may be unwel-
come to walkers but the combi-
nation of moisture and peat
bogs, formed by the degenera-
tion of ancient forests, provide
mosses, grasses and sedges
with a perfect home.

Opposite:
Blue skies: a pleasant reward
for the conquest of Pen yr Ole
Wen (3,209ft/978m) from the
Ogwen Valley. For those
attempting a traditional south-
north traverse of the Welsh
3,000ft peaks, this is perhaps
the most testing part of the
entire exercise coming, as it
does, immediately after the
knee-jarring descent of Tryfan
across the valley.

Right:
Late afternoon haze lends depth and mystery to this view of the Snowdonia hills from the summit plateau of Carnedd Llewelyn (3,491ft/1,064m) across the shoulder of Carnedd Dafydd (3,425ft/1,044m). The pointed peak of Elidir Fawr (3,031ft/924m) lies in the distance with Moel Eilio, a pale shadow behind.

Opposite:
Autumn sunlight and shadows on the ridge of Y Braich leading to Pen yr Helgi Du (*Hill of the Black Hound*) viewed from the north ridge of Tryfan. The reservoir road along the bottom provides easy access to Carnedd Llewelyn and Craig yr Ysfa, a favourite spot for rock climbers.

Left:
Walkers on the slopes of Carnedd Dafydd enjoy a fine October day traversing the Carneddau. In the background is the broad summit of Carnedd Llewelyn (3,491ft/ 1,064m) which physically dominates this exposed northern range in the same way that Llewelyn the Great (after which it was probably named) dominated local history.

Opposite:
Evening glow: looking eastwards from near the summit of Carnedd Llewelyn to the path that comes up from the reservoir road under Pen yr Helgi Du (right) and skirts round the summit rocks of Craig yr Ysfa. On the left is Pen Llithrig y Wrach.

Right:
This path along Cefn Ysgolion Duon (*Ridge of the Black Ladders*), together with the ridge of Bwlch Cyfryw-drum (far left distance), connects the two summits of Carnedd Dafydd and Carnedd Llewelyn. Never dropping below 3,000ft, it offers one of the best sustained high-level walks in Snowdonia. The cliffs (centre) plunging down into Cwm Llafar below are the Black Ladders themselves. Whilst damp and uninviting in summer, they make excellent climbing grounds in winter.

Left:
View from the summit slopes of Carnedd Dafydd towards Carnedd Llewelyn (3,491ft/1,064m, top left), the highest peak in the Carneddau range. Those attempting a traverse of all the Welsh 3,000ft peaks tend to contour the open slopes below Carnedd Llewelyn from Bwlch Cyfrywdrum in order to reach the outlying peak of Yr Elen (off left of picture) before ascending Carnedd Llewelyn. This avoids the need to climb Carnedd Llewelyn twice.

Opposite:
Yr Elen (3,156ft/962m) with Angelsey behind. Yr Elen (*Hill of the Fawn*) – one of the remotest Welsh 3,000ft peaks, and probably the least visited – lies half a mile northwest of Carnedd Llewelyn from whose summit it can be reached via a narrow ridge.

Right:
View from the western shoulder of Carnedd Llewelyn north towards Foel Fras (3,091ft/942m, centre) and Foel Grach (3,202ft/976m, right). The outlying rise on the left is Garnedd Uchaf (3,038ft/926m), a minor summit on the ridge joining these two peaks, which is now normally included in listings of the Welsh 3,000ft mountains.

Above left:
A perfect day out in the hills: Walking the skyline along Bwlch Cyfryw-drum, the ridge connecting Carnedd Llewelyn (3,491ft/1,064m) with Carnedd Dafydd (3,425ft/1,044m).

Below left:
Snow sculpted by the winds: a dry stone wall above the village of Gerlan on the west side of the Carneddau. Stone, together with slate, is the traditional building material throughout Gwynedd. The highly-skilled art of stone walling entails fitting together irregularly-shaped stones without having to cut them. Farmers examine their walls every spring for damage sustained during the winter.

Right:
View from the summit of
Carnedd Llewelyn across the
wild and remote upper reaches
of Cwm Eigiau towards Pen
Llithrig y Wrach (*Slippery Hill
of the Witch,* distant right).
Witches and magicians figure
prominently in the history and
folklore of North Wales, as this
delightful name suggests.

Opposite:
Lonely horizon: view from the
western edge of Carnedd
Llewelyn's summit towards Yr
Elen (3,156ft/962m) across
Ffynnon Caseg, one of
Snowdonia's smallest lakes,
which nestles in Cwm Caseg
(*The Mare's Hollow*). The
narrow ridge joining Yr Elen to
Carnedd Llewelyn runs along
the left edge.

Right:
A broody day on the remote northern slopes of Carnedd Llewelyn, suitably medieval in atmosphere: Welsh princes would often take refuge in the mountains during times of war and drive their flocks up out of the valleys to graze in the hills. This view north towards the outlying peaks of Foel Grach (3,202ft/976m), Garnedd Uchaf (3,038ft/926m) and Foel Fras (3,091ft/942m) marks the welcome end in sight of the traditional south-north traverse of the Welsh 3,000ft peaks.

Back cover:
Early winter snows on the shoulder of Carnedd Dafydd (3,425ft/1,044m) looking towards Carnedd Llewelyn (3,491ft/1,064m).